Gifts

to Make and Eat

Written by Elizabeth MacLeod
Illustrated by June Bradford

KIDS CAN PRESS

With lots of love to my parents-in-law, George and Helen Wilson

Text © 2001 Elizabeth MacLeod
Illustrations © 2001 Kids Can Press

KIDS CAN DO IT and the 📖 logo are trademarks of Kids Can Press Ltd.

Kids Can Press acknowledges the financial support of the Government of Canada, through the BPIDP, for our publishing activity.

Published in Canada by
Kids Can Press Ltd.
29 Birch Avenue
Toronto, ON M4V 1E2

Published in the U.S. by
Kids Can Press Ltd.
2250 Military Road
Tonawanda, NY 14150

www.kidscanpress.com

Edited by Lori Burwash
Designed by Karen Powers
Photography by Frank Baldassarra
Printed in Hong Kong by Wing King Tong Company Limited

The hardcover edition of this book is smyth sewn casebound.
The paperback edition of this book is limp sewn with a drawn-on cover.

CM 01 0 9 8 7 6 5 4 3 2 1
CM PA 01 0 9 8 7 6 5 4 3 2 1

Canadian Cataloguing in Publication Data

MacLeod, Elizabeth
Gifts to make and eat

(Kids can do it)
ISBN 1-55074-956-0 (bound)   ISBN 1-55074-958-7 (pbk.)

1. Cookery – Juvenile literature. 2. Gifts – Juvenile literature. 3. Gift wrapping – Juvenile literature.
I. Bradford, June. II. Title. III. Series.

TX652.5.M2418 2001   j641.5'123   C00-932860-2

Kids Can Press is a Nelvana company

Contents

Introduction 4

Chocolate Treats

Almond bark 6
Chocolate clusters 7
Truffle mice 8

Grab a Handful

Great granola 10
Party nibbles 11

Nutty Snacks

Trail mix 12
Sweet and spicy nuts 13

The Cookie Jar

Peanut butter cookies 14
Shortbread valentines 15
Gingerbread people 16
Quick cookie mix 18

Soup to Go

Layered soup mix 20
Onion soup mix 21

Fantastic Fudge

Butterscotch fudge 22
Stained-glass fudge 23

Spice It Up

Cinnamon toast mix 24
Italian seasoning 24
Green salad herbs 25
Mexi-spice 25
Super salt 25

Muffins and Loaves

Oatmeal muffins 26
Raisin loaf 27
Marvelous muffin mix 28

Dressing Up

Pizza oil 30
Just in thyme oil 30
Raspberry vinegar 31
Honey-sweet mustard 31

Sweet Treats

Creamy mints 32
Sweet strawberries 33

Gifts to Sip

Hot chocolate 34
Spicy citrus tea 35

Quick Picks

Chocolate pretzels 36
Chocolate spoons 36
Reindeer canes 37
Clementine wreath 37

It's a Wrap 38

Introduction

*Need to give a gift, but low on ideas —
and money? Here's a book full of
presents that are easy and inexpensive
to make and that taste great.*

*Whether your gift list includes a friend
with a sweet tooth, a gourmet
cook, a chocolate lover or a relative
who loves hiking, you'll find the perfect
present here. And by making and
decorating a reusable container or adding
an extra present, you'll create a unique
gift your friend can enjoy long after
the edible present is gone!*

MIXING AND MATCHING

Make a really terrific present by
combining ideas. Send the cookie mix
(page 18) and the muffin mix (page 28)
to someone who likes to bake. Package
together the green salad herbs (page 25)
and raspberry vinegar (page 31). What
other combos can you create?

You can also mix and match recipes
and wrapping ideas. Try putting the
muffin mix (page 28) in a resealable
plastic bag and slipping it into a paper
cone (page 21). Pick the containers and
decorations that you think your friends
or relatives would like best and use
their favorite colors.

MEASURING INGREDIENTS

Both the metric and imperial systems of
measurement are used in this book. The
systems are different, so choose one and
use it for all your measuring.

Wet ingredients and dry ingredients
require different measuring cups. A wet
measuring cup has a spout to make
pouring easier. A dry measuring cup is
flat across the top so you can use a knife
to level off the ingredients for an
accurate measure.

ABBREVIATIONS

The following metric and imperial abbreviations have been used:

L	=	liter
mL	=	milliliter
g	=	gram
°C	=	degrees Celsius
cm	=	centimeter
c.	=	cup
tbsp.	=	tablespoon
tsp.	=	teaspoon
lb.	=	pound
oz.	=	ounce
fl. oz.	=	fluid ounce
°F	=	degrees Fahrenheit
in.	=	inch

MELTING CHOCOLATE

Chocolate burns easily, so ask an adult to help you melt it in a microwave or double boiler. Heat chocolate slowly, just enough to melt it, stirring frequently. If using a microwave, stir the chocolate at least every 30 seconds. If using a double boiler, place it on low heat. You can melt chips, squares or bars — cut up bars to help them melt faster.

BAKING

Bake cookies, muffins and loaves in the center of your oven. Cooking times vary from oven to oven, so bake for the minimum time suggested, then check. Cookies are baked when lightly browned and firm to the touch. Muffins are done when you gently touch the middle of a muffin and it springs back. To check a loaf, insert a toothpick or cake tester into the middle. If it comes out clean and dry, the loaf is done. If your treat is not done, check it again in a few minutes — set a timer to remind you.

TOASTING NUTS AND COCONUT

Preheat oven to 150°C (300°F). Spread nuts on a baking sheet and place in the oven for 2 minutes. Wearing oven mitts, remove the sheet, stir the nuts and put back in the oven for 1 minute. Repeat until the nuts are lightly browned. Toast coconut for no more than 1 minute at a time.

> Use thick oven mitts to handle hot saucepans, baking sheets or cake pans. Ask an adult to help move things into and out of the oven.

> Make sure you don't give a present containing nuts to someone who is allergic to them. Also, carefully clean your utensils and work surface after making a recipe with nuts.

Almond bark

*Creamy chocolate and crunchy almonds
make a delicious combo.*

YOU WILL NEED

750 g	white chocolate, melted (page 5)	1½ lb.
500 mL	unblanched whole almonds, toasted (page 5)	2 c.

a large mixing bowl, a wooden spoon,
a baking sheet lined with wax paper

1 In the bowl, stir together the chocolate and almonds.

2 Pour the mixture onto the baking sheet. Spread it out just until none of the almonds touch.

3 Refrigerate for 1 hour or until firm. Break into pieces.

Store in an airtight container in a cool, dark place or in the fridge for up to 2 weeks.

Makes about 875 g (1¾ lb.) almond bark

OTHER IDEAS

♥ Pour melted dark or milk chocolate over Reese's Pieces or crushed candy canes, instead of almonds.

WRAP IT UP

♥ Cut a square of felt large enough to cover the sides of a margarine tub. Spread a thin layer of white glue on the sides of the tub, place it on the felt, and shape the felt around it. Hold with an elastic. Cut ribbon long enough to go around the top and put glue on its wrong side. Wrap the ribbon around the elastic and hold in place with another elastic until dry.

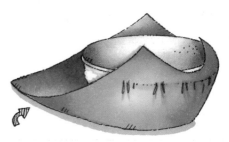

Chocolate clusters

It's hard to believe that a candy can be so simple to make, yet taste so good.

YOU WILL NEED

225 g	milk chocolate, melted (page 5)	8 oz.
250 mL	chopped nuts (any kind), toasted (page 5)	1 c.
250 mL	shredded coconut, toasted (page 5)	1 c.

a wooden spoon, a small spoon,
2 baking sheets lined with wax paper,
about 30 paper candy cups

1 Cool the melted chocolate for about 10 minutes.

2 Stir the nuts and coconut into the chocolate.

3 With the small spoon, place spoonfuls of the mixture on the baking sheets.

4 Refrigerate for 2 hours or until firm. Place one cluster each in a paper cup.

Store in an airtight container in the fridge for up to 1 month or in the freezer for up to 2 months.

Makes about 3 dozen clusters

WRAP IT UP

♥ Paint cardboard (not Styrofoam) egg cartons, inside and out. When dry, paint greetings or designs on the tops. Place a cluster (in its paper cup) in each cup of the carton.

Truffle mice

*These cute treats taste
even better than they look.*

YOU WILL NEED

4	28 g (1 oz.) squares semisweet chocolate, melted (page 5)	4
75 mL	sour cream	1/3 c.
300 mL	fine chocolate-wafer crumbs (about 30 cookies)	1¼ c.
24	silver dragées (small edible balls)	24
24	sliced almonds	24
12	short pieces black shoestring licorice	12

a large mixing bowl, a fork, measuring cups
and spoons, plastic wrap, a small plate,
a tray lined with wax paper

1 In the bowl, use the fork to mix the chocolate and sour cream.

2 Add 250 mL (1 c.) chocolate-wafer crumbs and mix well.

3 Cover the bowl with plastic and refrigerate for 1 hour or until firm.

4 Place the remaining chocolate-wafer crumbs on the plate.

5 With your fingers, form about 15 mL (1 tbsp.) of the chocolate mixture into a ball. Pinch one end to look like a mouse's nose.

6 Roll the pointed ball in the crumbs. Place it on the tray.

7 Repeat steps 5 and 6 with the rest of the mixture.

8 On each mouse, place two dragées near the pointed end for eyes, insert two almonds for ears, and add shoestring licorice for the tail.

9 Refrigerate for at least 2 hours or until firm.

Refrigerate in an airtight container for up to 1 week.

Makes 1 dozen mice

OTHER IDEAS

♥ Make white mice by rolling the mouse-shaped balls in 50 mL (¼ c.) icing sugar. Use gold dragées or small red candies for eyes and red shoestring licorice for tails.

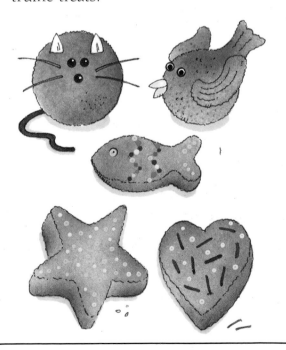

♥ Try molding the chocolate mixture into fish, cats or birds. Or make shapes such as stars, hearts or diamonds. Use any candies you like to decorate your truffle treats.

WRAP IT UP

♥ Cover the lid and bottom of a box with bright paper.

1. Cut a piece of paper at least 2 cm (¾ in.) larger around than the lid. Center the lid on the paper and glue it in place.

2. Fold the paper over the sides, making cuts at the corners. Glue down the edges of the paper. Repeat steps 1 and 2 with the bottom of the box, making sure the paper is large enough to cover the sides.

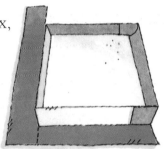

♥ If you like, cut a cat or mouse face out of construction paper and glue it on the lid. Put a napkin or Easter grass in the box and nestle the mice in it.

Great granola

Anybody who likes healthy treats will love this granola.

YOU WILL NEED

1 L	quick-cooking (not instant) oatmeal	4 c.
250 mL	shredded coconut	1 c.
250 mL	chopped pecans	1 c.
50 mL	oat bran	1/4 c.
10 mL	ground cinnamon	2 tsp.
1 mL	ground nutmeg	1/4 tsp.
pinch	salt	pinch
125 mL	liquid honey	1/2 c.
50 mL	vegetable oil	1/4 c.
5 mL	vanilla	1 tsp.
175 mL	raisins or dried fruit	3/4 c.

a large mixing bowl, a wooden spoon,
a medium saucepan,
2 lightly greased baking sheets

1 Preheat the oven to 160°C (325°F).

2 In the bowl, stir together the oatmeal, coconut, pecans, oat bran, cinnamon, nutmeg and salt.

3 Place the honey and oil in the saucepan and warm to a simmer, stirring occasionally. Remove from heat and stir in the vanilla.

4 Pour the honey mixture over the oatmeal mixture and stir.

5 Place granola on the baking sheets. Bake 15 to 20 minutes, until golden.

6 Cool for 30 minutes. Meanwhile, wash and dry the bowl.

7 Place the granola in the bowl and stir in the raisins or dried fruit.

Store in an airtight container for up to 1 month.

Makes 1.625 L (6½ c.) granola

WRAP IT UP

♥ Place some granola in a resealable plastic bag. Slip it into a gift bag decorated with stickers and ribbons.

Party nibbles

Whip up a batch of these nibbles for someone who likes to throw parties.

YOU WILL NEED

125 mL	butter or margarine	½ c.
1.25 L	corn and wheat cereal squares	5 c.
500 mL	oat ring cereal	2 c.
250 mL	pretzels	1 c.
25 mL	Worcestershire sauce	2 tbsp.
20 mL	garlic powder	4 tsp.
5 mL	celery salt	1 tsp.

a microwavable bowl or small saucepan, a wooden spoon, a large mixing bowl, 2 lightly greased baking sheets, paper towels

1 Preheat the oven to 120°C (250°F).

2 Ask an adult to help melt the butter in a microwave or on low heat on the stove. Stir every 20 seconds.

3 In the mixing bowl, stir together the cereals and pretzels. Add the remaining ingredients. Mix well.

4 Spread the mixture on the baking sheets. Bake 45 minutes, stirring every 15 minutes, until lightly browned.

5 Use the spoon to place the mixture on the paper towels to cool completely.

Store in an airtight container for up to 2 weeks.

Makes about 2 L (8 c.) nibbles

WRAP IT UP

♥ Put some nibbles in a resealable plastic bag. Cut a rectangle of felt slightly larger than the bag, then cut another rectangle the same size. Sew or glue the rectangles on three sides. Near the open end, cut eight evenly spaced slits and thread ribbon through. Drop the bag of nibbles in the felt bag, and tie the ribbon in a bow.

Trail mix

*Hikers and cross-country skiers will
love your homemade trail mix.*

YOU WILL NEED

250 mL	unsalted roasted sunflower seeds	1 c.
250 mL	raisins	1 c.
125 mL	dried pineapple, in large chunks	½ c.
125 mL	banana chips	½ c.
125 mL	unsalted roasted almonds	½ c.
125 mL	unsalted roasted cashews	½ c.
125 mL	unsalted roasted peanuts	½ c.

a large mixing bowl, a wooden spoon

1 In the bowl, mix together all the ingredients.

Store in an airtight container for up to 3 weeks.

Makes 1.125 L (4½ c.) trail mix

OTHER IDEAS

♥ Personalize the trail mix by substituting some of your friend's favorite dried fruits and nuts. Try diced papaya, cranberries, apricots, flaked coconut or green pumpkin seeds (pepitas).

WRAP IT UP

♥ Glue corrugated paper, wrapping paper or wallpaper around a canister or box. Then glue ribbon around the top and bottom. Glue a circle of the same paper to the lid, or cover it with a sticker. Pour some trail mix into a plastic bag, seal it tightly, and place it in the container.

Sweet and spicy nuts

This crunchy treat is a good present for when you're invited to a friend's or relative's for dinner.

YOU WILL NEED

75 mL	white sugar	⅓ c.
50 mL	butter	¼ c.
50 mL	orange juice	¼ c.
5 mL	salt	1 tsp.
5 mL	ground cinnamon	1 tsp.
1 mL	cayenne pepper	¼ tsp.
1 L	mixed, unsalted nuts	4 c.

a large saucepan, a wooden spoon,
a baking sheet lined with aluminum foil,
aluminum foil, a fork

1 Preheat the oven to 140°C (275°F).

2 In the saucepan, place the sugar, butter, orange juice, salt, cinnamon and cayenne. Over medium-low heat, stir until the sugar dissolves.

3 Increase heat to medium. Add the nuts and toss until well coated.

4 Spread the nuts on the baking sheet. Bake 90 minutes, stirring every 15 minutes.

5 Spread the nuts on a sheet of aluminum foil and use the fork to separate them. Cool completely.

Store in an airtight container for up to 2 weeks.

Makes 1 L (4 c.) nuts

WRAP IT UP

♥ Place some nuts on a large piece of cellophane and use ribbon to gather the ends together. Put the bundle in a bright plastic bowl. (If you want to wrap the nuts in a paper bag or box instead, put them in a resealable plastic bag first.)

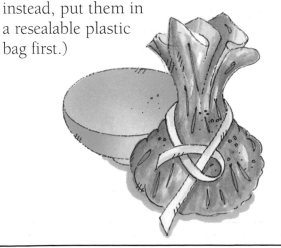

Peanut butter cookies

*Mmmm ... a great way to wish
a friend a happy birthday.*

YOU WILL NEED

250 mL	white sugar	1 c.
250 mL	peanut butter (a commercial brand, not natural)	1 c.
1	egg	1

a large mixing bowl, a wooden spoon,
a baking sheet lined with aluminum foil,
a fork, a lifter, a cooling rack

1 Preheat the oven to 180°C (350°F).

2 In the bowl, cream the sugar and peanut butter. Blend in the egg.

3 Form dough into balls about 2 cm (¾ in.) across. Place on the baking sheet and flatten with the fork. Bake 12 to 15 minutes, until golden.

4 Cool for 5 minutes, then use the lifter to transfer the cookies to the cooling rack to cool completely.

Store in an airtight container at room temperature for up to 1 week or in the freezer for up to 2 months. (Note: Make sure your friend isn't allergic to peanut butter.)

Makes about 2 dozen cookies

OTHER IDEAS

♥ Add 125 mL (½ c.) chocolate chips to the dough.

WRAP IT UP

♥ Decorate a canister by wrapping it with colored cord. Cover the bottom quarter of a canister with glue and wind on the cord. Continue up the canister, a quarter at a time, to just below the top, so the lid still fits.

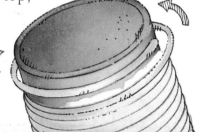

Shortbread valentines

These cookies will make anybody's Valentine's Day extra special.

YOU WILL NEED

500 mL	butter, at room temperature	2 c.
250 mL	brown sugar, lightly packed	1 c.
1 L	all-purpose flour	4 c.

a large mixing bowl, a wooden spoon,
wax paper, a rolling pin,
heart-shaped cookie cutters, a lifter,
a baking sheet lined with aluminum foil,
a cooling rack

1 Preheat the oven to 150°C (300°F).

2 In the bowl, cream together the butter and brown sugar. Add the flour and mix thoroughly.

3 Place the dough on a sheet of wax paper and roll it out with the rolling pin until it is about 0.5 cm (¼ in.) thick. Cut hearts with cookie cutters, and use the lifter to transfer them to the baking sheet.

4 Bake 12 to 15 minutes, until just cooked. The cookies should be very pale.

5 Cool for 5 minutes, then use the lifter to transfer the cookies to the cooling rack to cool completely.

Store in an airtight container at room temperature for up to 1 week or in the freezer for up to 2 months.

Makes about 5 dozen cookies

WRAP IT UP

♥ Stamp hearts on a box. Put cookies in the box with wax paper between layers. Add a cookie cutter, if you like.

Gingerbread people

A family will love these gingerbread people — and pets — that look like themselves.

YOU WILL NEED

175 mL	butter, at room temperature	¾ c.
125 mL	brown sugar, lightly packed	½ c.
1	egg	1
175 mL	molasses	¾ c.
750 mL	all-purpose flour	3 c.
10 mL	ground ginger	2 tsp.
7 mL	ground cinnamon	1½ tsp.
2 mL	ground nutmeg	½ tsp.
1 mL	salt	¼ tsp.

a large mixing bowl, a wooden spoon, wax paper, a rolling pin, gingerbread-people cookie cutters, a lifter, 2 baking sheets lined with aluminum foil, a cooling rack

1 In the bowl, beat together the butter and sugar until they are light and creamy.

2 Stir in the egg and molasses.

3 Add the remaining ingredients and blend well.

4 Divide the dough into two balls. Wrap each one in wax paper and refrigerate for 2 hours.

5 Preheat the oven to 190°C (375°F).

6 Unwrap one ball of dough and roll it out with the rolling pin on its wax paper until it is about 0.5 cm (¼ in.) thick. Cut gingerbread people with the cookie cutters. With the lifter, transfer the cookies to the baking sheets. Repeat with the other ball.

7 Bake 10 minutes, until firm. Cool for 5 minutes, then use the lifter to transfer the cookies to the cooling rack to cool completely.

8 Decorate with icing and candy.

Store in an airtight container at room temperature for up to 1 week or in the freezer for up to 2 months.

Makes about 2 dozen cookies

OTHER IDEAS

♥ Make gingerbread gift tags. Cut tags out of the rolled dough, and use a straw to poke a hole near one end before baking. Use icing to write a message on the tag, then tie the tag to your present with shoestring licorice.

♥ Gingerbread people also make great Christmas tree ornaments. With a straw, poke a hole near the top of each one before baking. Use ribbon to hang the decorations.

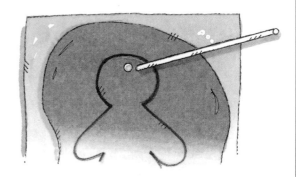

♥ Make a cookie-gram by rolling out a large rectangle of dough and baking it. When cool, write a message on it with icing.

WRAP IT UP

♥ Place a cookie inside a small, clear cellophane bag. If you like, first decorate the bag with stickers and other decorations. Tie the bag shut with ribbon.

Quick cookie mix

No time to bake? This cookie mix is easy to make and can be baked into different kinds of cookies and squares.

YOU WILL NEED

1 L	all-purpose flour	4 c.
1 L	white sugar	4 c.
375 mL	instant milk powder	1½ c.
22 mL	baking powder	1½ tbsp.
5 mL	salt	1 tsp.

2 large mixing bowls, a fork, a sifter

1 In one bowl, use the fork to mix all the ingredients together well.

2 Using the sifter and the other bowl, sift the mixture twice.

Store in airtight containers at room temperature for up to 4 weeks.

Makes 2 L (8 c.) mix

WRAP IT UP

♥ Cover the container with decoupage. Mix equal amounts of white glue and water, or buy decoupage glue. Dip pieces of colored paper or magazine pictures in the mixture. Smooth them onto the container. When the decoupage is dry, cover it with two coats of acrylic varnish. Let dry after each coat.

Give your friend a package of the mix with one or all of the following recipes. Print the recipes on colorful paper.

Chocolate chip cookies

1. Preheat oven to 180°C (350°F).

2. Mix 500 mL (2 c.) of this cookie mix with 75 mL (⅓ c.) melted butter or margarine. Add 1 lightly beaten egg and 10 mL (2 tsp.) vanilla, and stir. Add 150 mL (⅔ c.) chocolate chips. Mix well.

3. With lightly floured hands, shape batter into 2.5 cm (1 in.) balls, and arrange about 5 cm (2 in.) apart on a lightly greased baking sheet. Bake 8 to 10 minutes, until golden. Immediately remove from baking sheet to cooling rack.

Instead of chocolate chips, add raisins, chopped nuts or coconut.

Makes about 30 cookies

Oatmeal bars

1. Preheat oven to 180°C (350°F).

2. Mix 500 mL (2 c.) of this cookie mix, 375 mL (1½ c.) quick-cooking (not instant) oatmeal and 2 mL (½ tsp.) ground cinnamon. Add 1 lightly beaten egg. Stir in 175 mL (¾ c.) melted butter or margarine. Add 50 mL (¼ c.) cold water and 10 mL (2 tsp.) vanilla. Mix well.

3. Pat the mixture into a 23 cm (9 in.) square cake pan lined with aluminum foil. Bake 30 to 35 minutes, until golden. Remove from oven and place on cooling rack. When completely cool, cut into bars.

Makes about 2 dozen bars

Brownies

1. Preheat oven to 190°C (375°F).

2. Mix 500 mL (2 c.) of this cookie mix with 1 lightly beaten egg.

3. Stir in 75 mL (⅓ c.) melted butter or margarine. Mix in 125 mL (½ c.) chocolate chips, 125 mL (½ c.) chopped pecans or walnuts, 125 mL (½ c.) cocoa powder, 75 mL (⅓ c.) cold water and 10 mL (2 tsp.) vanilla.

4. Pour the batter into a foil-lined 20 cm (8 in.) square cake pan. Bake 25 minutes, until top springs back when touched and sides have shrunk away from pan. Remove from oven and place on cooling rack. When completely cool, frost with chocolate icing, if you like. Cut into squares.

Makes about 16 squares

Layered soup mix

This hearty soup is perfect for wintry afternoons.

YOU WILL NEED

125 mL	split peas	½ c.
125 mL	lentils	½ c.
125 mL	pearl barley	½ c.
125 mL	macaroni	½ c.
25 mL	parsley flakes	2 tbsp.
25 mL	dried chopped onion	2 tbsp.
5 mL	dried thyme	1 tsp.
2 mL	white pepper	½ tsp.

a clear jar with a tight-fitting lid,
a soup spoon

1 Place half the split peas in the bottom of the jar.

2 Use the spoon to carefully layer half the barley on top, then half the lentils and half the macaroni. Put all the parsley around the edge of the jar. Repeat the layers, but top with the onion flakes around the edge of the jar.

3 Sprinkle the thyme and pepper on top.

Store in an airtight container at room temperature for up to 2 months.

Makes 500 mL (2 c.) mix

Print these instructions on colorful paper and include with the soup mix:

Combine this soup mix with 2 L (8 c.) seasoned stock or water in a large, heavy saucepan. Bring to a boil. Reduce heat to low and cover. Simmer gently for 45 to 50 minutes, until split peas are tender.

WRAP IT UP

♥ Paint the jar's lid. When dry, wrap ribbon around its edge and cross the ends. Use a sticker to attach the ribbon to the jar. If you like, tuck dried herbs in the ribbon.

Onion soup mix

Any onion lover would love to receive this delicious soup mix.

YOU WILL NEED

175 mL	instant minced onion	¾ c.
75 mL	beef-flavor instant bouillon	⅓ c.
20 mL	onion powder	4 tsp.
5 mL	dried thyme	1 tsp.
1 mL	celery seed	¼ tsp.
1 mL	white sugar	¼ tsp.
a medium mixing bowl, a fork		

1 In the bowl, use the fork to combine all the ingredients.

Store in an airtight container at room temperature for up to 2 months.

Makes 300 mL (1¼ c.) mix

Print these instructions on colorful paper and include with the soup mix:

> Combine 50 mL (¼ c.) of this mix with 250 mL (1 c.) water in a saucepan. Heat on medium, stirring until hot.

WRAP IT UP

♥ Roll heavy paper or wallpaper into a large cone, using double-sided tape to fasten the edge. Punch holes in the cone and flap as shown, and thread ribbon through the holes in the cone. Place the soup mix in a resealable plastic bag and slip it into the cone. Fold down the flap and tie it closed with the ribbon.

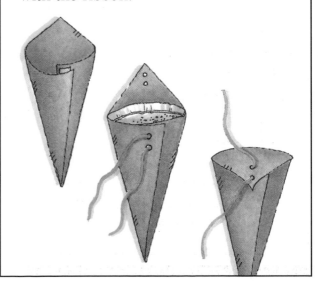

Butterscotch fudge

Make this delicious fudge for someone with a sweet tooth.

YOU WILL NEED

1	213 g (7½ oz.) jar marshmallow cream	1
1	160 mL (5 fl. oz.) can evaporated milk	1
250 mL	white sugar	1 c.
125 mL	butter	½ c.
2 mL	salt	½ tsp.
1	300 g (10 oz.) package butterscotch chips	1
125 mL	chopped pecans	½ c.
5 mL	vanilla	1 tsp.

a heavy saucepan, a wooden spoon,
a 20 cm (8 in.) square cake pan
lined with aluminum foil

1 In the saucepan, combine the marshmallow cream, milk, sugar, butter and salt.

2 With an adult's help, bring to a rolling boil over medium-low heat, stirring constantly. Boil for 5 minutes, continuing to stir.

3 Remove from heat and add the chips, pecans and vanilla. Stir until the chips are melted.

4 Pour fudge into pan. Refrigerate for 4 hours or until firm.

Refrigerate covered (with foil or plastic) for up to 2 weeks. (The fudge will keep better if you don't cut it until you give it away. When you do, remove from pan and cut into squares.)

Makes about 25 squares

WRAP IT UP

♥ Decorate a box with buttons, shells or beads. Leave enough room around the top so the lid still fits. Use white glue or a glue gun to attach them. Make sure the glue is completely dry before handling the box.

Stained-glass fudge

A bright, colorful treat!

YOU WILL NEED

675 g	white chocolate, broken into pieces	1½ lb.
1	300 mL (10 fl. oz.) can sweetened condensed milk	1
pinch	salt	pinch
375 mL	mini gumdrops, all colors except black	1½ c.
2 mL	vanilla	½ tsp.

a large microwavable bowl, a wooden spoon, a 23 cm (9 in.) square cake pan

1 In the bowl, combine the chocolate, milk and salt. Microwave on high for 3 to 5 minutes, stirring every 90 seconds, until the chocolate is melted. (You can also heat in a double boiler over medium-low heat [page 5].)

2 Stir in gumdrops and vanilla.

3 Pour fudge into pan. Refrigerate for 2 hours or until firm.

Refrigerate covered (with foil or plastic) for up to 2 weeks. (The fudge will keep better if you don't cut it until you give it away. When you do, remove from pan and cut into squares.)

Makes about 25 squares

WRAP IT UP

♥ Cut about 50 small squares of tissue paper. Brush decoupage glue (see "Wrap It Up" on page 18) over part of a clear plastic container. Place some squares on the glue so that they overlap slightly. Continue covering the container and let it dry. Spread on another layer of glue and let dry.

You'll find a spice mix here for every person on your list. The mixes taste best if used within six months.

Cinnamon toast mix

Sprinkle on toast, muffins or even cocoa.

YOU WILL NEED		
250 mL	white sugar	1 c.
15 mL	ground cinnamon	1 tbsp.

Mix the ingredients and store in an airtight container with a shaker lid.

Italian seasoning

Delicious on lasagna, cannelloni or pizza!

YOU WILL NEED		
25 mL	dried basil	2 tbsp.
25 mL	dried oregano	2 tbsp.
15 mL	dried minced parsley	1 tbsp.
15 mL	dried minced garlic	1 tbsp.
5 mL	dried rosemary	1 tsp.
5 mL	dried thyme	1 tsp.
2 mL	paprika	½ tsp.
2 mL	coarsely ground black pepper	½ tsp.

Mix all ingredients and store in an airtight container.

Green salad herbs

*Great for a vegetarian friend
or salad lover.*

YOU WILL NEED		
50 mL	dried minced parsley	¼ c.
25 mL	dried chopped chives	2 tbsp.
15 mL	dried thyme	1 tbsp.
15 mL	dried basil	1 tbsp.
10 mL	dried dill	2 tsp.
5 mL	dried tarragon	1 tsp.

Mix all ingredients and store in an
airtight container.

Mexi-spice

*Perfect for anyone who loves
spicy Mexican food.*

YOU WILL NEED		
45 mL	dried minced onions	3 tbsp.
22 mL	chili powder	1½ tbsp.
5 mL	salt	1 tsp.
10 mL	cornstarch	2 tsp.
10 mL	crushed dried red pepper	2 tsp.
10 mL	dried minced garlic	2 tsp.
10 mL	ground cumin	2 tsp.
5 mL	dried oregano	1 tsp.

Mix all ingredients and store in an
airtight container.

Super salt

*Sprinkle on popcorn or add to
vegetables, stews and soups.*

YOU WILL NEED		
125 mL	salt	½ c.
45 mL	garlic salt	3 tbsp.
5 mL	paprika	1 tsp.
2 mL	pepper	½ tsp.
2 mL	dried oregano	½ tsp.
1 mL	celery seed	¼ tsp.
1 mL	white pepper	¼ tsp.
1 mL	dry mustard	¼ tsp.

Mix all ingredients and store in an
airtight container with a shaker lid.

WRAP IT UP

♥ Arrange a few spice mixes in a
small basket.

♥ Wrap two small jars end to end in
cellophane or paper. Tie the ends with
ribbon and decorate with stickers.

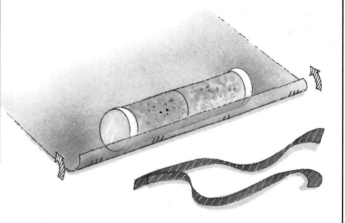

Oatmeal muffins

Try personalizing these muffins by adding a friend's favorite berries.

YOU WILL NEED

250 mL	quick-cooking (not instant) oatmeal	1 c.
250 mL	milk	1 c.
1	egg	1
50 mL	vegetable oil	¼ c.
250 mL	all-purpose flour	1 c.
125 mL	brown sugar, lightly packed	½ c.
15 mL	baking powder	1 tbsp.
2 mL	salt	½ tsp.

a large and a medium mixing bowl,
a wooden spoon, a cereal spoon,
a muffin pan lined with muffin papers,
a cooling rack

1 Preheat the oven to 220°C (425°F).

2 In the large bowl, combine the oatmeal and milk. Let stand for 15 minutes.

3 Add the egg and oil. Mix well.

4 In the medium bowl, mix the remaining ingredients. Add to the oatmeal mixture and stir until just moistened.

5 Spoon batter into the muffin papers so that each is two-thirds full. Bake 20 to 25 minutes, until golden.

6 Cool for 10 minutes, then remove the muffins from the pan and cool completely on the cooling rack.

Store in an airtight container at room temperature for up to 1 week or in the freezer for up to 2 months.

Makes about 1 dozen muffins

WRAP IT UP

♥ Line a clean flower pot with plastic wrap or cellophane and fill it with muffins. Gather the wrap and tie it with a bow. If you like, paint and decorate the flower pot before filling it.

Raisin loaf

Anyone with a dairy or egg allergy will appreciate this loaf.

YOU WILL NEED

300 mL	water	1¼ c.
250 mL	brown sugar, lightly packed	1 c.
250 mL	raisins	1 c.
125 mL	shortening	½ c.
5 mL	ground cinnamon	1 tsp.
2 mL	ground allspice	½ tsp.
2 mL	ground nutmeg	½ tsp.
500 mL	all-purpose flour	2 c.
5 mL	baking soda	1 tsp.
5 mL	baking powder	1 tsp.
2 mL	salt	½ tsp.

a medium saucepan,
a wooden spoon, a sifter, a loaf pan lined
with aluminum foil, a cooling rack

1 Preheat the oven to 180°C (350°F).

2 In the saucepan, combine the water, sugar, raisins, shortening and spices. With an adult's help, warm the mixture over medium heat until it boils. Boil for 5 minutes.

3 Refrigerate for about 30 minutes, until at room temperature.

4 Sift the remaining ingredients into the raisin mixture and stir well.

5 Pour batter into the pan. Bake 45 to 50 minutes, until firm.

6 Cool for 30 minutes, then remove from the pan and foil and cool completely on the cooling rack.

Wrap in plastic wrap and foil and store at room temperature for up to 1 week or in the freezer for up to 2 months.

Makes 1 loaf

WRAP IT UP

♥ Place the loaf in the center of a cloth napkin. Gather the corners of the napkin and hold in place with an elastic band. Use wide ribbon to tie a bow over the elastic.

Marvelous muffin mix

This mix makes enough for 4 dozen muffins, so divide it in half and give it to two friends!

YOU WILL NEED

1.25 L	all-purpose flour	5 c.
375 mL	white sugar	1½ c.
250 mL	whole wheat flour	1 c.
250 mL	instant milk powder	1 c.
50 mL	baking powder	¼ c.
15 mL	ground cinnamon	1 tbsp.
5 mL	salt	1 tsp.
2 mL	ground cloves	½ tsp.

2 large mixing bowls, a fork, a sifter

1 In one bowl, use the fork to mix all the ingredients together well.

2 Using the sifter and the other bowl, sift the mixture twice.

Store in airtight containers at room temperature for up to 4 weeks.

Makes 2 L (8 c.) mix

Print this recipe on colorful paper and include with the muffin mix:

---

1. Preheat oven to 200°C (400°F). Line 12 muffin cups with muffin papers.

2. To 500 mL (2 c.) of this muffin mix, add 150 mL (⅔ c.) water, 1 lightly beaten egg and 50 mL (¼ c.) vegetable oil. Stir until dry ingredients are just moistened. If you like, add 125 mL (½ c.) raisins, dates, chopped nuts or chocolate chips.

3. Fill muffin papers about half full. Bake 10 to 15 minutes, until done. Cool for 10 minutes, then remove muffins from pan and cool completely on cooling rack.

Makes 1 dozen muffins

WRAP IT UP

♥ Make an apron for each jar or bottle.

1. On scrap paper, draw an apron to fit your jar and cut it out.

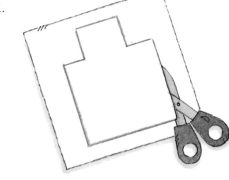

2. Punch two holes near the top and two at the waist. Knot string through each hole.

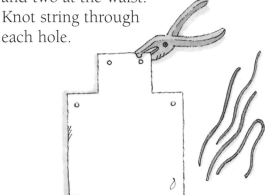

3. Carefully tie the pattern to the jar. Make the pattern larger or smaller as necessary.

4. When you have a pattern you like, use it to cut an apron out of felt or paper.

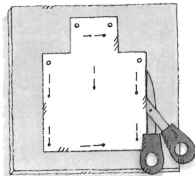

5. Add a pocket and tuck in the recipe. Use ribbon to tie the apron to the jar. If you like, paint the lid.

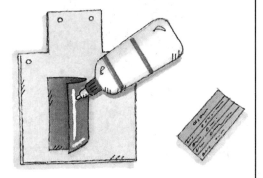

♥ To make your present extra special, attach a cooking utensil, such as a set of measuring spoons, or a bag of raisins, nuts or chocolate chips.

♥ If you want to send the mix to a far-away friend, pour it into a resealable plastic bag instead.

*Flavored oils, vinegars and mustards
are great presents for gourmet cooks.
They're best for people who live nearby,
because the bottles can break in mailing.*

Pizza oil

Drizzle over pizza for extra pizzazz.

YOU WILL NEED		
4	garlic cloves, halved	4
6	dried red chilies	6
1	large sprig fresh thyme	1
1	large sprig fresh rosemary	1
15 mL	whole peppercorns	1 tbsp.
500 mL	olive oil	2 c.

Thread the garlic cloves on a bamboo skewer. Place the skewer and remaining seasoning in a bottle (with lid). Pour in the oil and put on the lid. Store in a cool, dark place for 1 week before giving.

Just in thyme oil

Give this oil to someone who makes her own salad dressings.

YOU WILL NEED	
2	large sprigs fresh thyme 2
	olive oil (enough to fill bottle)

Put the thyme in a bottle (with lid). Pour in enough olive oil to almost fill the bottle. Put on the lid. Store in a cool, dark place for 10 days before giving.

Raspberry vinegar

Great in dressings for green salads that include fruit.

YOU WILL NEED		
500 mL	raspberries	2 c.
1 L	white vinegar	4 c.

Put 8 berries aside. Heat remaining berries and vinegar in a large saucepan on low for 15 minutes. Do not let the mixture boil. Meanwhile, fill a bottle (with lid) with warm water.

When vinegar is heated, empty the bottle. Strain the vinegar into a large measuring cup, then pour into the bottle. Add the 8 raspberries and put on the lid. Store in a cool, dark place for 1 week before giving.

OTHER IDEAS

♥ Make herb vinegar by pouring warm vinegar into a bottle containing a few sprigs of a fresh herb, such as thyme or rosemary. Store in a cool, dark place for 1 to 2 weeks, then strain and add fresh sprigs before giving.

Honey-sweet mustard

Sweet, spicy and delicious.

YOU WILL NEED		
125 mL	dry mustard	½ c.
50 mL	liquid honey	¼ c.
25 mL	brown sugar, lightly packed	2 tbsp.
25 mL	red or white wine vinegar	2 tbsp.
1 mL	ground cloves	¼ tsp.
1 mL	salt	¼ tsp.

Combine all ingredients in a bowl and blend with a fork until smooth. Store in a jar, refrigerating for at least 1 day before giving. (This mustard should be kept in the fridge.)

WRAP IT UP

♥ Draw designs on the bottles with dimensional fabric paint. You can also add a tag describing what's inside.

Creamy mints

Mints are a great gift any time of year.

YOU WILL NEED

500 mL	icing sugar	2 c.
60 g	cream cheese, softened	2 oz.
24	drops peppermint flavoring	24
12	drops green food coloring	12
24	small candies (optional)	24

a large mixing bowl, wax paper,
a rolling pin, small cookie cutters

1 In the bowl, use your hands to blend the icing sugar and cream cheese until completely mixed.

2 Work the flavoring through the dough.

3 Knead in the food coloring.

4 Place the dough between two pieces of wax paper and roll it with the rolling pin until it is about 1 cm (½ in.) thick.

5 Cut dough with the cookie cutters. Decorate each mint with a small candy, if you like.

Refrigerate in an airtight container, with wax paper between the layers, for up to 2 weeks. (Include a note telling your friend to keep the mints in the fridge.)

Makes 2 dozen mints

WRAP IT UP

♥ Paint or stain a wooden or paper box and glue on fabric braid or other trim. Dab a little glue on the ends to keep them from fraying.

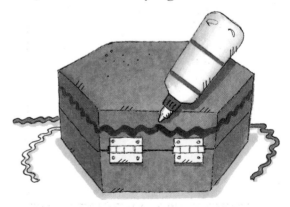

Sweet strawberries

Celebrate summer with these delicious treats.

YOU WILL NEED

1	170 g (6 oz.) package strawberry gelatin powder	1
500 mL	shredded coconut	2 c.
175 mL	sweetened condensed milk	¾ c.
16	drops green food coloring	16
25 mL	sliced blanched almonds	2 tbsp.
50 mL	red-colored sugar	¼ c.

a large mixing bowl, a wooden spoon, plastic wrap, a glass plate (or any plate that won't absorb food coloring), a fork, wax paper, a small spoon

1 In the bowl, mix together the gelatin powder and coconut. Add the milk and stir well.

2 Cover the dough with plastic wrap and refrigerate for 1 hour.

3 Meanwhile, pour the food coloring on the plate and add the almonds. Stir them with the fork until they are dark green, then place on a piece of wax paper to dry completely.

4 With the small spoon, scoop up some dough and, with your fingers, mold it into a strawberry shape. Sprinkle the sugar onto some wax paper and roll the berry in it. Repeat with the remaining dough.

5 Insert two almonds at the flat end of each berry to make leaves.

Store in an airtight container, with wax paper between the layers, at room temperature for up to 1 week or in the fridge for up to 2 weeks.

Makes about 3 dozen strawberries

WRAP IT UP

♥ Weave ribbon through the sides of a plastic berry basket. Use cellophane and ribbon to wrap your gift.

Hot chocolate

A tasty, soothing gift for a cold day.

YOU WILL NEED

500 mL	instant milk powder	2 c.
175 mL	white sugar	¾ c.
125 mL	coffee whitener powder	½ c.
125 mL	cocoa powder	½ c.

2 large mixing bowls, a sifter,
a wooden spoon

1 In one bowl, use the sifter to sift all the ingredients. Mix well.

2 Repeat step 1, sifting into the other bowl.

Store in an airtight container at room temperature for up to 2 months.

Makes about 925 mL (3 ¾ c.) mix

Print this note on colorful paper and include with the hot chocolate mix:

> To make a cup of hot chocolate, place 75 mL (⅓ c.) of this mix in a mug, add 250 mL (1 c.) boiling water and stir well.

OTHER IDEAS

♥ Sift 15 mL (1 tbsp.) ground cinnamon into the mix for a spiced hot chocolate mix.

♥ Add 250 mL (1 c.) miniature marshmallows.

WRAP IT UP

♥ Place some mix in a cellophane bag and slip it into a mug. Decorate with ribbon and other decorations, if you like.

Spicy citrus tea

*This spicy, sweet drink makes
a delicious present.*

YOU WILL NEED

325 mL	orange drink powder	1⅓ c.
250 mL	instant tea mix	1 c.
10 mL	ground cinnamon	2 tsp.
5 mL	ground cloves	1 tsp.

2 large mixing bowls, a sifter,
a wooden spoon

1 In one bowl, use the sifter to sift all the ingredients. Mix well.

2 Repeat step 1, sifting into the other bowl.

Store in an airtight container at room temperature for up to 2 months.

Makes about 575 mL (2⅓ c.) mix

Print this note on colorful paper and include with the tea mix:

> To make a cup of tea, place 22 mL (1½ tbsp.) of this mix in a mug, add 250 mL (1 c.) boiling water and stir well.

WRAP IT UP

❤ Pour the tea mix into a jar, then make a cap for it. Cut a piece of bright paper or fabric (use pinking shears so fabric won't fray) about 5 cm (2 in.) larger around than the lid. Screw on the lid, put the cap over it, and hold in place with an elastic. Cover the elastic with ribbon.

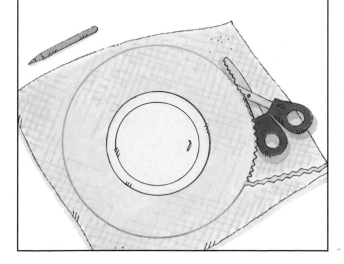

Chocolate pretzels

1 Dip one end of a pretzel rod in melted white, milk or dark chocolate (page 5).

2 Stand the pretzel — chocolate end up — in a glass for about 10 minutes, until the chocolate has hardened a little. Roll it in candy sprinkles, mini chips, nuts or crushed candy canes. Let stand until completely hardened.

3 Repeat for as many pretzels as you like. Wrap each pretzel separately in wax paper.

OTHER IDEAS

♥ Dip candy sticks or candy canes the same way.

Chocolate spoons

1 Dip a plastic spoon in melted chocolate (page 5). Make sure the bowl of the spoon is completely covered.

2 Stand the spoon — chocolate end up — in a glass for about 1 hour, or refrigerate for 30 minutes, until the chocolate has hardened.

Wrap a dozen spoons — some dipped in white, some in milk and some in dark chocolate — with a mug and the hot chocolate mix (page 34).

OTHER IDEAS

♥ Dip dried apricots, pineapple rings, dates or other dried fruit in melted chocolate (page 5). Place the dipped fruit on wax paper until the chocolate has hardened.

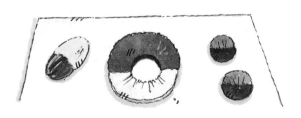

Reindeer canes

1 Onto plastic-wrapped candy canes, glue roly eyes, a black pompom nose and a rickrack or felt tie.

2 Twist a pipe cleaner around the curve in the cane to make antlers.

OTHER IDEAS

♥ Make a team of reindeer. Use a red pompom nose for Rudolph. Add felt ears and a different tie or scarf to each reindeer.

Clementine wreath

1 Cut a piece of transparent cellophane about 142 cm x 30 cm (56 in. x 12 in.).

2 Arrange 10 clementine oranges down the middle of the cellophane, with the first one about 23 cm (9 in.) from one end. The clementines should be about 5 cm (2 in.) apart, with the last one about 23 cm (9 in.) from the other end. Wrap the cellophane around them.

3 Tie a small bow between each clementine and at both ends.

4 Tie the ends of the cellophane together with a big bow.

It's a Wrap

Whether you're giving a gift to a friend down the street or a relative across the country, it will look even better when you decorate it and package it carefully. You'll find ideas for wrapping and decorating throughout the book. Here are more, as well as tips to make sure your gift arrives in good shape.

WRAP IT

♥ Cover a clean milk carton or ice cream tub with aluminum foil. Using white glue, squirt on designs, such as stripes or squiggles. Sprinkle glitter on the wet glue, then shake off any excess glitter.

♥ Paint over any writing on a jar lid with thick poster or latex paint, or cover it with a large round sticker or several small stickers.

♥ Decorate a container with stamps. Soak stamps off envelopes, then dry them between paper towels, under heavy books, for a few hours. Glue the stamps to your container. If you don't have enough stamps to cover it completely, paint it first with thick poster or latex paint or cover with paper.

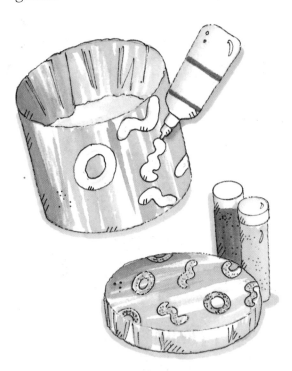

TAG IT

♥ Use computer clip art to design cards and tags. Print out black-and-white illustrations and color them.

♥ Place a cookie cutter on light cardboard or construction paper and trace around it. Cut out the shape and punch a hole to thread ribbon through.

♥ Cut tags from corrugated paper. Decorate the front and write on the back.

♥ Cut small designs from cards or wrapping paper and glue them onto larger plain tags.

DRESS IT UP

♥ If your present is in a can, stick fridge magnets to the side of the can.

♥ Use neon shoelaces, hair ribbons or shoestring licorice to tie up your gift.

♥ Paint the outside of a mug with permanent enamel paints.

♥ Write out the recipe of the gift on a recipe card or scroll of paper and include it with the present.

♥ Stamp or stencil designs on plain paper bags.

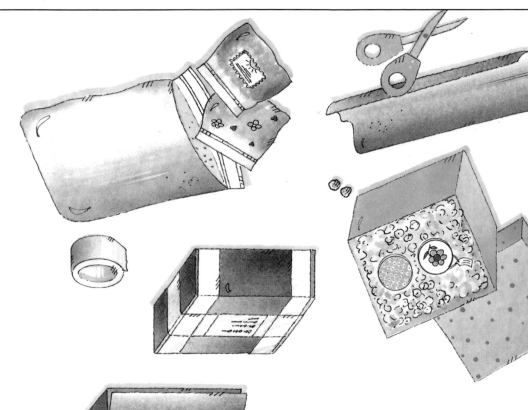

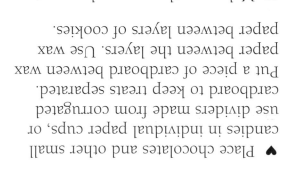

MAIL IT

♥ Place chocolates and other small candies in individual paper cups, or use dividers made from corrugated cardboard to keep treats separated. Put a piece of cardboard between wax paper between the layers. Use wax paper between layers of cookies.

♥ Make sure the wrapped present can't move around in its container. Pack newspaper, foam peanuts, tissue paper, bubble wrap or even popcorn around it. Stuff foam peanuts or shredded paper into small plastic bags to make it easy to unpack.

♥ Don't force a present into a box that's too small. Your gift will travel better in a slightly larger box stuffed full of packing material.

♥ Use strong tape to seal the box and its wrapping.

♥ Write the destination and return addresses clearly, and cover with clear tape so the ink doesn't run.

♥ You can mail non-breakable gifts — such as herb, cookie or muffin mixes in resealable plastic bags — in padded envelopes.

♥ Include a label with the destination and return addresses inside the parcel in case the outside wrapping is damaged.